Now I Know! 2

Speaking and Vocabulary Book

Kirstie Grainger

Contents

1 What do we do on school days?

Unit overview

▶ **Why do you like some subjects a lot?**

▶ **Do you learn more at school or at home?**

▶ **How important is it to learn art at school?**

Classes
art
computer science
drama
English
geography
math
P.E.
science
swimming
....
....

Other
guitar practice
piano practice
violin practice
....
....

Feelings
bored
tired
worried

Ways to describe activities
busy
difficult
easy
interesting
important

Az My new words

making a model ....

Vocabulary builder

1 Complete the chart for you.

> English   music   art   P.E.
>
> computer science   science   math

I have these classes today ...	I don't have these classes today ...

2 Match the words to the pictures.

a guitar practice

b swimming

c geography

d drama

3 Can you think of any more school words? Add them to the organizer on page 2.

4 What do you think? Answer.

What is your favorite class at school?

Do you like ... ?

My favorite class is ...

Yes, I do./ No, I don't.

Speaking 1

Why do you like some subjects a lot?

1 **Listen and check (✔).**
01

| | Why do you like this class? | | | |
What classes do you like best?	It's challenging.	It's fun.	It's interesting.	I'm good at it.
English				
science				
music				
drama				

2 **What do you think? Copy the table from Activity 1 in your notebook and complete with new subjects for yourself.**

3 **What do others think? Share your chart with a friend.**

What classes do you like? Why?

I like ... because ...

4 **What do you think now? Check (✔) the answers you agree with.**

I like classes that are fun. ◯

I like classes that are challenging. ◯

I like classes that are interesting. ◯

I like classes that I'm good at. ◯

 Find out about

What classes do you want to be better at? How can you improve?

Speaking strategy

Keep your hands away from your face when speaking.

Speaking 2

Do you learn more at school or at home?

1 Point and say what they're doing. Circle the activities you do at home.

2 How can these activities help you learn? Think and check (✔).
Can you add another activity?

	... helps me practice skills.	... helps me learn new information.
Watching TV		
Playing with my friends		
Reading a book		
Playing a computer game		
Cooking		
Making a model		

3 What do others think? Share your chart with a friend.

> Do you learn more at home or school?

> I think I learn more at ...

4 What do you think now? Circle.

I think I learn more at **home** / **school**.

Speaking 3

How important is it to learn art at school?

1   **Which art activities do you do at school? Can you add more?**

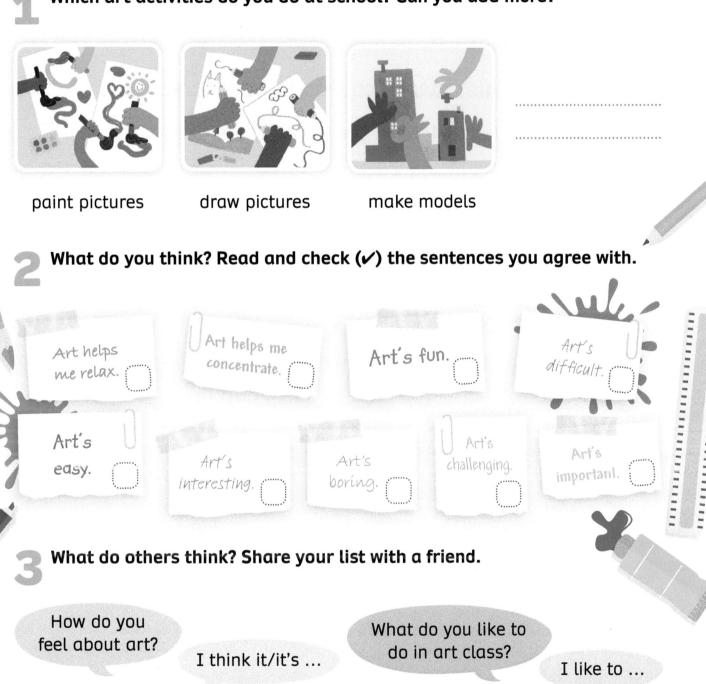

paint pictures   draw pictures   make models

....

....

2   **What do you think? Read and check (✔) the sentences you agree with.**

Art helps me relax. ☐

Art helps me concentrate. ☐

Art's fun. ☐

Art's difficult. ☐

Art's easy. ☐

Art's interesting. ☐

Art's boring. ☐

Art's challenging. ☐

Art's important. ☐

3   **What do others think? Share your list with a friend.**

> How do you feel about art?

> I think it/it's …

> What do you like to do in art class?

> I like to …

4   **What do you think now? Circle and write.**

1   My friend **likes / doesn't like** doing art at school because ....

2   I **think / don't think** art is important because ....

6

2 Where do wild animals live?

▶ **How do animals get their food?**

▶ **How do animals' special characteristics help them?**

▶ **What wild animals live in your country?**

Animals	Ways to describe animals or people
camel cheetah giraffe kangaroo lion monkey owl panda penguin seal snake zebra	angry dangerous fat funny lazy smart strong thin

Az My new words

claws ....

Vocabulary builder

1 Complete the chart. Use the words in the box. Can you add more animals?

seal	crocodile	kangaroo	panda	snake	whale

legs	no legs

2 🎧 **02** Look and circle. Then listen and check your answers.

1   monkey / giraffe   3   zebra / penguin   5   owl / zebra

2   owl / penguin   4   lion / monkey   6   giraffe / lion

3 Can you think of any more animals? Add them to the organizer on page 7.

4 What do you think? Answer.

What is your favorite wild animal?

Does it have legs/wings?

It's a ...

Yes, it does./No, it doesn't.

Speaking 1

How do animals get their food?

1 **Match the animals to their food.**

2 **What do you think? Check (✔) the body parts used to get their food.**

	hands	beak	teeth	claws
owls				
monkeys				
penguins				
lions				

3 **What do others think? Share your chart with a friend.**

How do ... get their food?

They use their ...

4 **What do you think now? Choose two animals. Then write.**

1 I think .... use their .... to get their food.

2 I think .... use their .... to get their food.

💬 **Speaking strategy**

Be open to others by not crossing arms in front of you.

Speaking 2

How do animals' special characteristics help them?

1 **What special characteristics does a polar bear have? Look and write the numbers.**

1   Thick, white fur helps keep it warm.

2   Strong legs help it swim.

3   Big, flat feet help it walk on snow and ice.

4   Sharp teeth help it eat meat.

2 **What do you think? Use the words in the box to find the animals. Write.**

| giraffe | camel | monkey | seal | kangaroo | crocodile |

1   A long tail helps it climb trees. ....

2   Big legs help it jump. ....

3   A long neck helps it eat leaves from tall trees. ....

4   Flippers help it swim. ....

5   A green body helps it hide in the water. ....

6   Thick fur keeps it cool in the desert. ....

3 **What do others think? Think of an animal. Talk about your animal with a friend.**

My animal is a ...

Does it have ... ?

... keep/keeps it warm/cool.

Yes, it does./ No, it doesn't. It has ...

4 **What do you think now? Draw your animal and tell a friend about a special characteristic that it has.**

Speaking 3

What wild animals live in your country?

1 Which habitats are in your country? Check (✔).

ocean

beach

desert

river

mountain

savannah

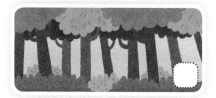

forest

jungle

outback

2 What do you think? What animals live in these habitats? Choose two habitats and write.

habitats in my country	some animals that live there

3 What do others think?

What animals
live in/on ... ?

... live in/on ...

 Find out about

Describe your favorite wild animal. Where does it live? How does it get its food?

4 What do you think now? Tell a friend about three animals that live in your country.

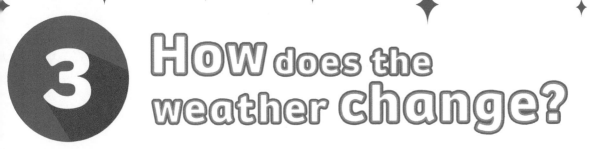

3 HOW does the weather change?

Unit overview

▶ **What do you do when you're too hot or too cold?**

▶ **How does water fall from the sky where you live?**

▶ **What do you do in different weather?**

Weather	Clothes and accessories
fog/foggy	cap
hail	pajamas
lightning	rain boots
rain	robe
sleet	scarf
snow	slippers
storm	sneakers
thunder	snow pants
tornado	sweat suit
wind/windy	woolly hat/socks
	....
	....

Az My new words

shade ....

Vocabulary builder

1 Complete the chart. Use the words in the box.

wind	sneakers	rain	cap	slippers	lightning
snow	sweat suit	woolly socks	rain boots	hail
scarf	thunder	sleet	flip flops	sunglasses	fog
robe	woolly hat	pajamas	snow pants

weather	things people wear

2 🎧 03 Listen and number.

3 Can you think of any more clothes or accessories words? Add them to the organizer on page 12.

4 What do you think? Answer.

What are you wearing?

I'm wearing ...

Do you like rain/snow?

Yes, I do./ No, I don't.

Speaking 1

What do you do when you're too hot or too cold?

1 **Read and match. Then say what he/she is doing.**

1 sit in the shade
2 drink a hot drink
3 drink cold water
4 put on a scarf
5 put on slippers
6 take off a sweater

2 **What do you think? Complete the chart for you. Use phrases from Activity 1 and add more.**

When I'm too hot, I ...	When I'm too cold, I ...

3 **What do others think? Share your chart with a friend.**

What do you do when you're too ... ?

When I'm too ... , I ...

4 **What do you think now? Write things you and your friend both do.**

1 When we're too hot, we ....

2 When we're too cold, we ....

Speaking 2

How does water fall from the sky where you live?

1 Point and say. Use the words in the box.

> It's snowing.   It's hailing.   It's sleeting.   It's raining.

2 What do you think? Check (✔) the answers for where you live.

	Do we have rain?	Do we have snow?	Do we have sleet?	Do we have hail?
Yes – a lot				
Yes – a little				
No				

3 What do others think? Compare your chart with a friend.

> Do we have … where we live?

> Yes, a lot./Yes, a little./ No, we don't.

4 What do you think now? Write a true sentence using *we have a lot of*, *we have a little*, or *we don't have*.

Where I live, we have a lot of snow.

Speaking 3

What do you do in different weather?

1 **Match and say. Then circle the pictures of activities you like to do.**

ride a bike

play on the playground

go skiing

go fishing

go swimming

make a snowman

2 **What do you think? Write.**

1 When it's sunny, I like to ....
2 When it's windy, I like to ....
3 When it's rainy, I like to ....
4 When it's snowy, I like to ....

3 **What do others think? Compare your answers in Activity 2 with a friend.**

What do you like to do when it's ... ?

Do you like to ... when it's ... ?

Yes, I do./No, I don't. I like to ...

I like to ... when it's ...

4 **What do you think now? Write things you both like to do.**

When it's ... , we like to ...

 Find out about

What's your favorite weather?
Why do you like it?

4 What can you find in big cities?

Unit overview

▶ What can you hear from your window?

▶ Do you need a car where you live?

▶ Where do you and your friends go to have fun?

Places in a town	Outside big cities
airport bank bookstore bus station clothes store factory library market movie theater parking lot playground restaurant sports center swimming pool toy store train station	fields small town street traffic

A_z My new words

play outdoors ....

17

Vocabulary builder

1 Read and circle.

1 People sometimes have dinner in a **bookstore / restaurant**.

2 There is lots of money in a **bank / playground**!

3 You can buy dolls at a **toy store / library**.

4 You can watch movies at the **movie theater / toy store**.

5 Children play with their friends on **restaurants / playgrounds**.

6 There are lots of books in a **movie theater / library**.

2 🎧 04 Listen and number. Then write. Use the words in the box.

| parking lot | bus station | sports center | airport | clothes store |

3 Can you think of any more places in a town? Add them to the organizer on page 17.

4 What do you think? Answer.

What are your favorite places near where you live?

Can you buy things/ play in a ... ?

My favorite places are ...

Yes, you can./ No, you can't.

Speaking 1

What can you hear from your window?

1 Look at the picture. Circle the things that make sounds.

2 What do you think? Go to the window. Check (✔) the things you can hear.

people		animals		machines		other	
shouting	◯	birds singing	◯	cars	◯	wind	◯
playing	◯	dogs barking	◯	factory	◯		

3 What do others think? Go to the window and compare with a friend.

> What can you hear?

> I can hear ...

Speaking strategy

Smile to show interest.

4 What do you think now? Write things that you can both hear.

We can hear ....
....
....

 Find out about

What can you hear from your window at home? How are sounds at home different from school?

Speaking 2

Do you need a car where you live?

1 **How do you travel? Point and say.**

go by car

go by bike

walk

go by train

go by bus

go by tram

go by subway

go by boat

2 **What do you think? Imagine four places and write.**

1 I go by .... to ....

2 I walk to ....

3 I ....

4 ....

3 **What do others think? Ask a friend.**

How do you travel to … ?

I go to (the) … by … /
I walk to (the) …

4 **What do you think now? Where do you travel by car? Write.**

I go by car to …	Can you travel a different way? How?

Speaking 3

Where do you and your friends go to have fun?

1 **Point and say the places where you go for fun. Then add and draw one more.**

park

clothes store

movie theater

sports center

playground

....

2 **What do you think? Write a place where each child can go.**

1 I like to buy clothes.

....

2 I like to play outdoors.

....

3 I like to watch movies.

....

4 I like to watch planes.

....

5 I like to look at books.

....

6 I like to have dinner with friends.

....

7 I like to play sports.

....

3 **What do others think? Ask a friend.**

Why do you go to the ... ?

I go to the ... because ...

4 **What do you think now? Write.**

We both go to these places for fun:

....

....

5 HOW do we celebrate?

Unit overview

▶ **Do you eat special food at celebrations?**

▶ **What makes celebrations special?**

▶ **Do we all celebrate the same things?**

Party food
burger
cupcake
milkshake
popcorn
fruit salad

Birthday things
balloon
candle
card

Fun places to visit
adventure playground
aquarium
bowling alley
climbing wall
ice rink
nature center
outdoor ski slope
theater
theme park
water park
zoo
....
....

Az My new words

tacos ....

22

Vocabulary builder

1 **Find and write six fun places to visit.**

1 ....   3 ....   5 ....

2 ....   4 ....   6 ....

2 **Match the words to the pictures.**

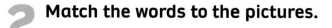

a climbing wall   **b** water park   **c** outdoor ski slope   **d** zoo   **e** theater

3 **Can you think of any more fun places to visit? Add them to the organizer on page 22.**

4 **What do you think? Answer.**

Would you like to go to ... ?

Is there a/an ... where you live?

Yes, I would./ No, I wouldn't.

Yes, there is./ No, there isn't.

Speaking 1

Do you eat special food at celebrations?

1 Use the code to write the names of the foods.

A	B	C	D	E	F	G	H	I	J	K	L	M	N	O	P	Q	R	S	T	U	V	W	X	Y	Z
1	2	3	4	5	6	7	8	9	1̲	2̲	3̲	4̲	5̲	6̲	7̲	8̲	9̲	1̄	2̄	3̄	4̄	5̄	6̄	7̄	8̄

1 2̄ 1 3 6̄ 1̄

2 6 9̲ 9 5 1̄

3 5̲ 6̄ 6 4 3̲ 5 1̄

4 7̲ 1 5̲ 3 1 2̲ 5 1̄

5 7 1 1̄ 2̲ 9 9 5 1̄

2 What do you think? Think of some foods that people eat at celebrations in your country. Write the words in code for a friend to solve.

3 What do others think? Ask a friend.

4 What do you think now? Draw two special foods from your country and write their names.

When do you eat ... in your country?

We normally eat ... at ...

Speaking 2

What makes celebrations special?

1 **Look at the picture. Count and write the numbers. Check your answers with a friend.**

How many people are ...

1 eating? .....

2 drinking? .....

3 playing guitars? .....

4 in the street parade? .....

5 watching fireworks? .....

2 **What do you think? Think of a celebration that you enjoy. Then check (✔) the things that you do.**

We have special food and drink. ☐

We wear special clothes. ☐

We dance. ☐

We have a street parade. ☐

We give and get presents. ☐

We have fireworks. ☐

We .... ☐

3 **What do others think? Ask some friends.**

What's your favorite celebration?

My favorite celebration is ...

💡 **Find out about**

What special events do you celebrate with your family?

4 **What do you think now? Write about your favorite celebration.**

My favorite celebration is ...
It's special because ...

Speaking 3

Do we all celebrate the same things?

1 Listen and circle the name of the special day. Then check (✔) the pictures of special days that you celebrate.

Easter / Eid

Carnival / Eid

Christmas / Carnival

New Year / Christmas

New Year / Easter

2 What do you think? Think of more special days that people celebrate around the world. Write.

special days that I celebrate	special days that I don't celebrate

3 What do others think? Ask a friend.

Who do you celebrate ... with?

I celebrate with ...

4 What do you think now? What special days do both you and your friend celebrate?

We both celebrate ....

....

....

6 What jobs can I do?

Unit overview

▶ **Do you only enjoy what you're good at?**

▶ **How do adults help you?**

▶ **What do people wear at work?**

Jobs	Actions
bus driver	cook
crossing guard	clean
dentist	study
doctor	fix
farmer	help
fire fighter	check
hairdresser	perform
mechanic	whistle
nurse	
photographer	
police officer	
sales clerk	
vet	
....	
....	

A_z My new words

fixing things ....

Vocabulary builder

1 Complete the crossword and find the mystery job. Use the words in the box.

mechanic   photographer   astronaut   dentist   chef   doctor

Mystery job:
....

2 🎧 06 Look and write. Then listen and check your answers.

sales clerk
nurse
farmer
bus driver
crossing guard
fire fighter

1 ....

3 ....

5 ....

2 ....

4 ....

6 ....

3 Can you think of any more jobs? Add them to the organizer on page 27.

4 What do you think? Answer.

I think a ... has an interesting/ important/difficult job.

Speaking 1

Do you only enjoy what you're good at?

1 Match the words to the pictures.

a speaking English	c climbing
b drawing	d cleaning

e dancing g fixing things

f singing

2 What do you think? Complete the chart. Use the phrases from Activity 1 and add more.

	I like …	I don't like …
I'm good at …		
I'm not good at …		

3 What do others think? Compare your chart with a friend.

What are/aren't you good at?

I'm quite good at …

4 What do you think now? Which things do you like doing best? Circle.

I like doing things I'm **good at** / **not good at** best.

 Speaking strategy

Think about tips in the earlier units to show interest.

Find out about

What things would you like to be better at? How can you improve?

Speaking 2

How do adults help you?

1 Look and circle the adults who are helping people. Then say.

2 What do you think? Think of the jobs of two adults who help you. Then circle and check (✔).

	job 1	job 2
He / **She** helps me learn things.		
He / **She** keeps me healthy.		
He / **She** keeps me safe.		
He / **She** helps me travel.		

3 What do others think? Compare your chart with a friend.

Who keeps you safe?

A police officer and crossing guard keep me safe.

4 What do you think now? Choose two jobs and write how they help you.

1 A .... helps me

   ....

2 A .... helps me

   ....

Speaking 3

What do people wear at work?

1 Point and say the jobs. Then check (✔) the people who are wearing a uniform.

2 What do you think? Draw people doing two different jobs and wearing the clothes that they wear at work.

3 What do others think? Share your pictures with a friend.

> He/She is wearing a uniform. What's his/her job?

> I think he/she must be a ...

4 What do you think now? Write two lists.

some jobs with uniforms	some jobs without uniforms

7 Why do we play sports?

Unit overview

▸ **What do you need to play sports?**

▸ **Is it important for sports to have rules?**

▸ **How can you be good at sports?**

Sports	Sports actions
baseball	bounce
field hockey	catch
horseback riding	hit
ice skating	hold
paddle boarding	kick
skateboarding	throw
skiing	....
track and field	....
volleyball	
water polo	
....	
....	

A_Z My new words

coach ....

Vocabulary builder

1 **Read and fill in the missing letters to make sports words.**

1 You wear this when you go paddleboarding. l __ f __ __ a __ k __ t
2 You play this sport with a stick and a ball. __ __ __ __ d h __ __ __ __ y
3 You play this sport with a small bat and a very small ball. __ i __ g – __ o __ g
4 You play this sport in water, with a ball. __ t __ r __ __ __ __ o
5 You wear this on your head when you go swimming. s __ __ __ __ __ __ n g __ __ p
6 You can do this when it snows in the mountains. s k __ i __ g

2 **Look at the pictures and complete the sentences using sports words.**

I like doing _____ .

I like going _____ .

I like playing _____ .

I like going _____ .

3 **Can you think of any more sports or sports actions? Add them to the organizer on page 32.**

4 **What do you think? Answer.**

What do you wear when you play/go/do … ?

When I play/go/do … , I wear …

Speaking 1

What do you need to play sports?

1 🎧 **07** **Listen and match.**

a people to play with

b a place to practice

c a time to practice

d equipment

e a coach

2 **What do you think? Think about a sport that you play. Answer the questions.**

| Who do you play with? | Where do you play? | When do you play? | What equipment do you need? | Do you have a coach? |

3 **What do others think? Ask some friends. Find out about different sports.**

4 **What do you think now? Write notes about a sport that a friend plays.**

What equipment do you need when you play ... ?

I/We need ...

Who do you play ... with?

I play ... with ...

Who with? ....

Where? ....

When? ....

Equipment? ....

Coach? **Yes / No**

 **Speaking strategy**

Nod your head to show agreement.

Speaking 2

Is it important for sports to have rules?

1 **Read and match the rules to the sports.**

1   You hit the ball over a net using a racket.   a   soccer

2   You kick the ball but you can't use your hands.   b   water polo

3   You hit the ball using a bat.   c   horseback riding

4   You throw and catch the ball and play in the water.   d   baseball

5   You have to wear a helmet to stay safe.   e   tennis

2 **What do you think? Look at the pictures. Circle the children who are following the rules.**

3 **What do others think? Share your ideas from Activity 2 with a friend. Use the words in the box to help you.**

| hold | kick | take off |
| run | throw | |

What's he/she doing?

He's/She's …

4 **What do you think now? Circle.**

I think rules **are** / **aren't** important in sports.

 Find out about

What is your favorite sport? Write the rules. What can and can't you do?

Speaking 3

How can you be good at sports?

1 **Complete. Use the words in the box.**

coach	hard	practice	equipment	fun	team

How can I be good at sports?

1 Try ....

2 Work as a ....

3 Have ....

4 Listen to the ....

5 Remember your ....

6 Go to every ....

2 **What do you think? Complete the chart. Use the phrases from Activity 1.**

very important ✔✔	important ✔	not important ✗

3 **What do others think?**

Is it important to ... ?

Yes, it's (very) important./No, it isn't important.

Do you ... when you play ... ?

Yes, I do./ No, I don't.

4 **What do you think now? How can you be better at sports? Write.**

When I play .... , I need to ....

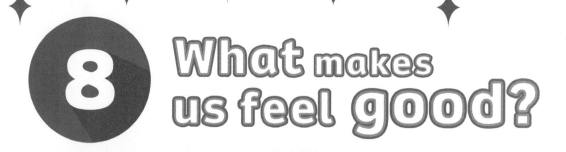

8 What makes us feel good?

Teeth words	Senses	Words to describe objects
braces chew dirty mouthwash rinse toothache toothbrush toothpaste	smell taste touch	rough soft smooth
	Actions	
	breathe feel hurt relax	

Az My new words

have energy ....

Vocabulary builder

1 **Write. Use the words in the box.**

| rinse | chew | smell | braces | tastes | relax |

1 Those cupcakes .... delicious!

2 I like to .... on my bed.

3 It's important to .... your food.

4 I wear .... because my teeth aren't straight.

5 I brush my teeth, then I .... my mouth out.

6 This mouthwash .... bad!

2 **Look and circle.**

1 This stone feels **rough / smooth**.

3 This hat feels **hard / soft**.

5 This bag feels **heavy / light**.

2 This stone feels **rough / smooth**.

4 This helmet feels **hard / soft**.

6 This bag feels **heavy / light**.

3 **Can you think of any more senses? Add them to the organizer on page 37.**

4 **What do you think? Describe objects in the classroom.**

How does this ... feel?

It feels ...

Speaking 1
Does candy make you feel good?

1 🎧 **Listen and number.**
08

2 **What do you think? Color the correct face for you.**

How do you feel when ...		
1 you eat too much candy?	☺	☹
2 you have your favorite candy?	☺	☹
3 your friends have more candy than you?	☺	☹
4 you share your candy?	☺	☹

3 **What do others think? Compare with a friend.**

Do you like candy?

Yes, I do./ No, I don't.

How do you feel when ... ?

I feel good/bad/ happy/sad.

4 **What do you think now? Write.**

1 My friend and I both feel good when ....

2 We both feel bad when ....

💬 **Speaking strategy**

Look at the speaker to show interest.

Speaking 2

What smells make you happy?

1 **Match the phrases to the pictures.**

a   garbage

b   freshly cut grass

c   fresh bread

d   the ocean

e   traffic

f   popcorn

2 **What do you think? Complete the chart. Use the phrases from Activity 1 and add more.**

I like these smells	I don't like these smells

3 **What do others think? Compare your chart with a friend.**

Do you like the smell of ... ?

Do you feel happy when you smell ... ?

Yes, I do./ No, I don't.

What's your favorite smell?

4 **What do you think now? Write.**

These smells make us both happy:

....

 Find out about

What sounds make you happy? Do you prefer loud sounds or quiet sounds?

Speaking 3

Do you like feeling healthy?

1 **How can you be healthy? Write *should* or *shouldn't*.**

If you want to be healthy ...

1 you .... eat lots of fruit and vegetables.

2 you .... eat lots of candy.

3 you .... get lots of exercise.

4 you .... go to bed late.

5 you .... get enough sleep.

2 **What do you think? How healthy are you today? Answer *yes* or *no*.**

1 Do you feel sick? ....

2 Do you feel strong? ....

3 Are your teeth clean? ....

4 Do you feel tired? ....

5 Do you have lots of energy? ....

3 **What do others think? Share with a friend.**

Do you feel sick/feel strong/feel tired/have lots of energy today?

Yes, I do./ No, I don't.

4 **What do you think now? Circle.**

1 When I feel sick, I feel **good** / **bad**.

2 When I feel strong, I feel **good** / **bad**.

3 When my teeth are clean, I feel **good** / **bad**.

9 HOW are the seasons different?

Unit overview

▶ **Do you need night-time to sleep?**

▶ **What is your favorite season like?**

▶ **What important events happen every year?**

Months	Time and place	Seasons
April	hour	fall
August	minute	spring
December	north	summer
February	second	winter
January		
July	....	
June	....	
March		
May		
November		
October		
September		

A_z My new words

daytime ....

Vocabulary builder

1 Find and circle the months. Then draw lines and write the months in order.

BKSAPRILGFEBRUARYMOLJUNECNARMAYUD(JANUARY)FHYZMARCHRIEJ

1	JANUARY	**3**	....	**5**	....
2	....	**4**	....	**6**	....

PSEPTEMBEROSUTJDECEMBERFDCARJULYBLNOVEMBERGAUGUSTKOCTOBER

7	....	**9**	....	**11**	....
8	....	**10**	....	**12**	....

2 Read the sentences and circle the answers with a friend.

1	There are 24 hours in	**a**	a day.	**b**	a month.
2	There are 12 months in	**a**	a day.	**b**	a year.
3	There are 7 days in	**a**	a year.	**b**	a week.
4	There are 60 minutes in	**a**	an hour.	**b**	a second.
5	There are 52 weeks in	**a**	a minute.	**b**	a year.
6	There are 60 seconds in	**a**	a minute.	**b**	a day.

3 Can you think of any more time or place words? Add them to the organizer on page 42.

4 What do you think? Ask a friend.

How many ... are in a ... ?

A ... is longer than a ...

Which is longer, a ... or a ... ?

Which months have ... days?

Speaking 1

Do you need night-time to sleep?

1 Write the sentences on the correct side of the world.

> It's dark.   It's light.   It's daytime.   It's night-time.

....

....

2 Choose a phrase from each box. Write three sentences that are true for you.

It's easy		when it's dark.
It's difficult	to wake up	when it's light.
I like	to sleep	in the daytime.
I don't like		at night.

3 What do others think? Ask a friend.

> Is it easy to wake up/sleep when it's dark/light?

> Yes, it is./No, it isn't.

4 What do you think now? Write *always*, *often*, *sometimes*, or *never*.

1 I .... sleep at night.

2 I .... sleep in the daytime.

 **Speaking strategy**

Ask questions to find out more.

💡 **Find out about**

Do babies sleep in the daytime? How many hours do they sleep at night?

Speaking 2

What is your favorite season like?

1 🎧 **Which season do these children like best? Listen and write. Use the words in the box.**
09

| spring | summer | fall | winter |

1 .... 2 .... 3 .... 4 ....

2 **What do you think? Write your favorite season and check (✔) the sentences that describe it. Add one more.**

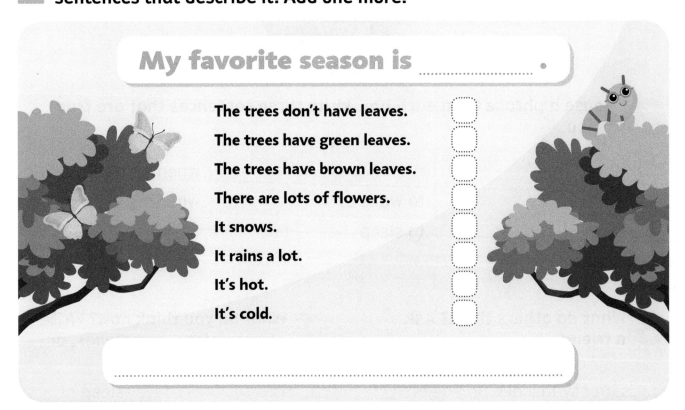

My favorite season is .... **.**

The trees don't have leaves. ☐

The trees have green leaves. ☐

The trees have brown leaves. ☐

There are lots of flowers. ☐

It snows. ☐

It rains a lot. ☐

It's hot. ☐

It's cold. ☐

....

3 **What do others think? Ask a friend.**

What's the weather like in your favorite season?

It/It's …

4 **What do you think now? Write what you like most about your favorite season.**

I like .... because ....

Speaking 3

What important events happen every year?

1 **Look at the pictures and write the correct number next to the word. Then tell a friend what they're doing.**

vacation ( )   start school ( )   birthday ( )   Christmas ( )

In picture 1, they're having a birthday party.

2 **What do you think? When do important events happen in your country? Write two sentences.**

In my country, we start school in January.

1 ....

2 ....

3 **What do others think? Talk to a friend.**

Do you go on vacation/start school/celebrate ... in ... ?

Yes, I do./ No, I don't.

4 **What do you think now? Write.**

The three most important events in my year are:

1 ....

2 ....

3 ....

10 How are we all different?

▶ **How do you and your friend look similar or different?**

▶ **Can you have friends who are older or younger than you?**

▶ **What are you like?**

Personality (how someone acts)	Appearance (how someone looks)
active chatty creative grumpy hardworking helpful kind nervous practical shy	eyebrows beard mustache bald blonde straight ....

Az My new words

....

47

Vocabulary builder

1 Complete the crossword. Use the words in the box.

straight   beard   eyebrows   curly
mustache   blonde   bald   wavy

2 Read and circle.

1   He always smiles. He's very **nervous** / **cheerful**.

2   He makes me laugh. He's **serious** / **funny**!

3   He always says "please" and "thank you". He's very **polite** / **practical**.

4   She can't relax. She's **nervous** / **funny**.

5   She doesn't often smile. She's very **serious** / **polite**.

3 Can you think of any more words to describe personality or appearance? Add them to the organizer on page 47.

Does your dad/uncle/ grandfather have a beard/mustache?

4 What do you think? Answer.

Yes, he does./ No, he doesn't.

Speaking 1

How do you and your friend look similar or different?

1 Describe your hair and your friend's hair. Use words in the box to help you.

> brown   blonde   red   black   wavy
> curly   straight   long   short

I have long, straight, black hair. My friend has blonde, curly hair.

2 What do you think? Read the questions and check (✔) the correct answer.

Me and 😊 😊 my friend

1 Who is taller?	Me. ☐	My friend. ☐
2 Who has longer hair?	Me. ☐	My friend. ☐
3 Who has darker hair?	Me. ☐	My friend. ☐
4 Who has bigger eyes?	Me. ☐	My friend. ☐
5 Who has longer legs?	Me. ☐	My friend. ☐

3 What do others think? Compare your answers with your friend's.

> I'm taller/shorter than you.

> Yes, I agree./ No, I don't think so.

4 What do you think now? Write about how you and your friend are similar and different.

 Find out about

How do people in your family look similar or different?

 Speaking strategy

Disagree politely.

Speaking 2

Can you have friends who are older or younger than you?

1 Read about Billy. Which friends are older than him and which friends are younger? What is the age difference between him and them?

Hi, my name is Billy. I'm 8. These are my best friends. This is Alex. He's 10. He's very tall! This is Aisha. She's 15. She has curly hair. This is Fay. She's very helpful. She's 7.

2 What do you think? Choose four friends. Complete the chart with their names and ages.

	friend 1	friend 2	friend 3	friend 4
name				
age				

3 What do others think? Share your chart with a friend.

> How old is your best friend?

> He's/She's …

> Is … older or younger than you?

> He's/She's older/younger than me.

4 What do you think now? Check (✔) the sentence(s) you agree with.

1 We can have friends who are older.

2 We can have friends who are younger.

3 All of our friends should be the same age.

Speaking 3
What are you like?

1 🎧 **10** **What is Anna like? Listen and check (✔).**

active	☐	funny	☐	nervous	☐
brave	☐	grumpy	☐	polite	☐
chatty	☐	hardworking	☐	practical	☐
cheerful	☐	helpful	☐	serious	☐
creative	☐	kind	☐	shy	☐

2 **What do you think? Write words from Activity 1 in the chart about you.**

I'm very …	I'm quite …	I'd like to be more …

3 **What do others think? Compare your chart with a friend.**

> I think you're …
> Do you agree?

> Yes, I think I'm very/quite … /
> No, I'm not./I don't think so.

> Would you like
> to be more … ?

> Yes, I would./
> No, I wouldn't.

4 **What do you think now? Write.**

1 I think I'm very _____ .

2 I think I'm quite _____ .

3 My friend thinks I'm _____ .

11 How do we solve problems?

Unit overview

▶ **When do you use math?**

▶ **How do you feel about math?**

▶ **How can you solve problems?**

Math	Problem-solving
equals	clue
measure	entrance
minus	exit
plus	hide
problem	lost
score	maze
subtract	solve
....	treasure hunt
....	

A_z My new words

....

Vocabulary builder

1 **Read and match the problems to the answers.**

1	Add three and three. The answer is	**a** nine.
2	Ten minus two equals	**b** five.
3	Five plus four equals	**c** six.
4	Subtract one from eight. The answer is	**d** two.
5	Add four and one. The answer is	**e** eight.
6	Six minus four equals	**f** seven.

2 **Look and complete. Use the words in the box.**

money   half   count   points   score

1 The _____ is 3–2!

2 Let's _____ . 1, 2, 3, 4 …

3 I have five _____ !

4 This is my _____ .

5 I have _____ the candies.

3 **Can you think of any more math words? Add them to the organizer on page 52.**

4 **What do you think? Talk to a friend.**

What's seven plus/minus one?

What's half of six?

Let's count to ten.

One, two, three …

Speaking 1

When do you use math?

1 🎧 **11** **Listen to the conversations and write the correct number in the boxes.**

go shopping ⬭

play sports ⬭

play computer games ⬭

cook ⬭

share candy ⬭

2 **What do you think? Check (✔). Then add one more.**

I use math ...	often	sometimes	never
1 when I go shopping			
2 when I share candy			
3 when I play sports			
4 when I play computer games			
5 when I cook			
6			

3 **What do others think? Ask a friend.**

Where do you use math?

I sometimes/often/always use math at home/at school/ in stores.

4 **What do you think now? Write.**

My friend and I both use math when

....

 Find out about

Look around and find numbers on signs. What do they mean?

 Speaking strategy

Take turns describing something.

54

Speaking 2

How do you feel about math?

1 **Match the words to the pictures.**

a counting money **b** doing math **c** measuring something **d** solving a word problem **e** doing a number puzzle

2 **What do you think? Check (✔) the sentences you agree with.**

I like counting things. ⬚

I like measuring things. ⬚

I like solving word problems. ⬚

I like doing number puzzles. ⬚

I like math when it's challenging. ⬚

I like math when it's easy. ⬚

3 **What do others think?**

How do you feel when you do math?

I feel happy/sad/bored/interested.

4 **What do you think now? Write. Use phrases from Activity 2.**

1 I don't like ....

....

2 I like ....

....

Speaking 3

How can you solve problems?

1 **Look and complete the sentences. Use the words in the box.**

map	adult	think	internet	book	talk

1 .... to your friends.

2 Look on the ....

3 Ask an .... for help.

4 Look at a ....

5 Look in a ....

6 Stop and ....

2 **What do you think? Write advice for each child. You can use ideas from Activity 1.**

> I want to do this puzzle but it's too difficult!

> This crossword is difficult! What's this word?

1 Why don't you .... ?   3 Why don't you .... ?

> We can't find the sports center!

> I want to make a paper plane.

2 Why don't you .... ?   4 Why don't you .... ?

3 **What do others think?**

> What can you do if you need/want to ...

> You can ...

4 **What do you think now? Tell a friend.**

My favorite ways of solving problems are ...

56

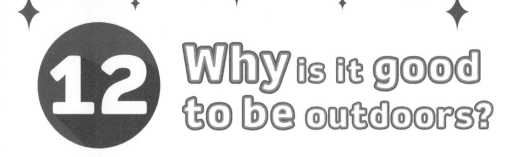

12 Why is it good to be outdoors?

Unit overview

- What did you do outdoors yesterday?
- What can you do in your favorite outdoor place?
- What things do you use when you go outdoors?

Outdoors	Vacations
cave	air mattress
cliff	fins
hills	hotel
island	sandcastle
lake	seaweed
meadow	shell
mud	snorkel
pond	water wings
rock	
stream	
waterfall	
wildlife	
....	
....	

Az My new words

....

Vocabulary builder

1 **Unscramble and write the words.**

1 dlwiflei ....

2 ksrco ....

3 sgsar ....

4 dnpo ....

5 lihsl ....

6 nsda ....

7 oadwme ....

8 elka ....

2 **Look and circle.**

1 island / cave

3 cave / stream

5 island / stream

2 mud / waterfall

4 cliff / waterfall

6 cliff / mud

3 **Can you think of any more outdoors words? Add them to the organizer on page 57.**

4 **What do you think? Answer.**

Do you like playing in the mud/in streams?

Yes, I do./ No, I don't.

Would you like to visit a dark cave?

Yes, I would./ No, I wouldn't.

Speaking 1

What did you do outdoors yesterday?

1 🎧 12 **Listen and check (✔) the things that Katie did outdoors yesterday.**

2 **What do you think? Write about things you did outdoors yesterday. Use the words in the box to help you.**

| walked | cycled | talked | played | visited | climbed |

Yesterday, I ...

3 **What do others think? Ask a friend.**

What did you do outdoors yesterday?

I walked home from school.

Did you climb a tree?

Yes, I did./ No, I didn't.

4 **What do you think now? Write.**

Yesterday, my friend and I both ....

Speaking 2

What can you do in your favorite outdoor place?

1 Point and say what the children are doing.

2 What do you think? Check (✔) the activities you can do at your favorite outdoor place. Add one more.

learn about wildlife	☐	play sports	☐	climb	☐
take pictures	☐	cycle	☐	swim	☐
play with my friends	☐	walk	☐	....	☐
collect things	☐	run	☐		

3 What do others think? Talk to a friend.

> Can you ... in your favorite outdoor place?

> Yes, I can./ No, I can't.

4 What do you think now? Write.

When I go to my favorite outdoor place, I often ....
....

💬 **Speaking strategy**

Take turns speaking.

💡 **Find out about**

Describe an outdoor place you often visit with your family.

Speaking 3

What things do you use when you go outdoors?

1 Check (✔) the things people use when they are outdoors.

rain boots ⬚   camera ⬚   jacket ⬚   snorkel ⬚

toothbrush ⬚   TV ⬚   bed ⬚   ball ⬚

map ⬚   backpack ⬚

2 What do you think? Complete the chart with things you use outdoors. Use words from Activity 1 to help you. Add more.

often	sometimes	never

3 What do others think? Compare your chart with a friend.

> Do you use ... outdoors?

> What else do you use outdoors?

> Yes/No, I sometimes/often/ never use ... outdoors.

> I sometimes/often use ...

4 What do you think now? Draw and write.

Pearson Education Limited
KAO TWO
KAO Park
Hockham Way
Harlow
Essex CM17 9SR
England
and Associated Companies throughout the world.

www.English.com

ISBN: 978-1-292-21938-7

Set in Daytona Pro Primary 13pt over 15.6pt

Eighth impression 2023

Printed and bound by CPI Group (UK) Ltd, Croydon, CRO 4YY

Image Credit(s):
123RF.com: Highwaystarz 3, Lisafx 5, Fotokostic 5, Mhgallery 8, Selivanov Lurii 20, Wavebreakmediamicro 23, Rez_art 24, Olegdudko 24, Dream04 24, Wang Tom 26, Dhalamov 26, Dglimages 26, Sergey Novikov 33, Tuan Nguyen 36, Servickuz 38, Patrick J Hanrahan 40, Shaman1006 44, Rob Marmion 46, Gpointstudio 46, Choreograph 55, Anyka 58; **Getty Images:** Inmagineasia 26; **Pearson Education Ltd:** Miguel Domingues Munz 18, Coleman Yuen 18, 20, Gareth Boden 58; **Shutterstock.com:** MBI 3, 20, B Calkins 3, Wavebreakmedia 3, BestPhotoPlus 5, Tetra Images 5, Africa Studio 5, Samuel Borges Photography 5, Irina Sokolovskaya 8, Stephen Lavery 8, Volodymyr Goinyk 8, EcoPrint 8, Paul Banton 8, Zhiltsov Alexandr 10, Swa182 15, Nebojsa Markovic 15, FamVeld 15, Romrodphoto 15, 23, Andreas Altenburger 18, Zhu Difeng 18, Tyler Olson 18, LightField Studios 20, Tzido Sun 20, Rawpixel.com 20, Leonid Andronov 20, Natalia Bratslavsky 20, Jbor 23, Lapandr 23, Karnizz 23, Svry 24, Jreika 24, Val Thoermer 26, Simez78 33, Sirtravelalot 33, NadyaEugene 33, Howard Sandler 38, Kedrov 38, Nielskliim 38, Marcos Mesa Sam Wordley 38, Morrowlight 38, PhawKStudio 40, Bochkarev Photography 40, Gunter Nezhoda 40, Sergey Ryzhov 40, Ssuaphotos 40, Amble Design 46, Gorillaimages 46, Pressmaster 55, Anna Hoychuk 55, Daniel Gale 55, Djem 55, Regien Paassen 58, Jarno Gonzalez Zarraonandia 58, Peter Clark 58, Veniamin Kraskov 58.

Cover Images: *Front:* **Getty Images:** Cavan Images

All other images © Pearson Education

Illustrations by: Barbara Bakos (The Bright Agency) pp.8, 11, 13, 16, 18, 21, 23, 31, 33, 36, 41, 58, 61; Camilla Galindo (Beehive Illustration) pp15, 27, 30, 32, 37, 50, 55, 62.